Mother Gave a Shout

Poems by women and girls

Edited by Susanna Steele and Morag Styles

Illustrated by Jane Ray

A&C Black · London

A CIP catalogue record for this book is available
from the British Library

ISBN 0-7136-3242-9

© 1990 A & C Black (Publishers) Limited

Published by A&C Black (Publishers) Ltd
35 Bedford Row, London WC1R 4JH

Filmset by August Filmsetting, Haydock, St Helens
Printed in Great Britain at the St Edmundsbury Press
Bury St Edmunds, Suffolk

Contents

Introduction

We started collecting the poems in *Mother Gave a Shout* several years ago, with young people of 9–13 in mind. Since then, we've discovered that many of the poems appeal to people of all ages.

The title *Mother Gave a Shout* comes from the well known rhyme 'One, two, three, mother caught a flea'. The book is divided into nine sections. **Here I am!** opens the book with girls and women writing about themselves; **O Dearie Me!** includes traditional, clapping and playground rhymes, played and passed on by girls; **The Moon and the Stars Above, And the Earth Beneath** feature poems about the natural world; **For Grandma's Sake Hush up** draws on lullabies old and new; **Telling Tales** includes songs, ballads and stories; **Wha Me Mudder Do** is about what mothers and grandmothers do, sometimes from the point of view of the adult, sometimes from the child's; and at the end, **Hold Fast your Dreams** includes reflections on our world, while **A New Day Dawning** closes with hopes for the future.

Mother Gave a Shout celebrates a wide range of girls' and women's voices in poetry, voices that have not always been heard. Poets writing in Britain today are set in the company of other times, as far back as Ancient Greece and China, and other cultures, as widespread as contemporary Aboriginal Australia and Black South Africa. This is poetry for everyone. It was a great pleasure to work on this book: we hope you enjoy it as much as we do.

Susanna Steele   Morag Styles

Here I am

Protest Poem

See ME
Look!
I am
here
I am
here
I am
here.

Pamela Mordecai
(extract)

Thumbprint

On the pad of my thumb
are whorls, whirls, wheels
in a unique design:
mine alone.
What a treasure to own!
My own flesh, my own feelings.
No other, however grand or base,
can ever contain the same.
My signature,
thumbing the pages of my time.
My universe key,
my singularity.
Impress, implant,
I am myself,
of all my atom parts I am the sum.
And out of my blood and my brain
I make my own interior weather,
my own sun and rain.
Imprint my mark upon the world
whatever I shall become.

Eve Merriam

When I am angry
I feel something inside of me angry
too.
That thing cries;
I cry.
When it's hungry,
I am hungry.
So when it dies
I die.
That thing is part of me.

Trang Ly*

You Say

You say I am mysterious.
Let me explain myself:
In a land of oranges
I am faithful to apples.

Elsa Gidlow

The Photograph

In a photograph of myself
I look like somebody else
Just when I laughed
the photographer snapped the picture
and in the photograph I'm laughing
exactly the way I was
when the photographer snapped it

Even so, I look like somebody else
in the photographer's picture

Siv Widerberg

My Life

I am Cheryl the Peril, I'm proud to relate
I know what I like
and
I know what I hate.
I hate rainy days and wet afternoons
I hate cars and yellow balloons
I like making friends and the buzz of a bee
HEY, I like being ME!

*Cheryl**

529 1983

Absent-mindedly,
Sometimes,
I lift the receiver
And dial my own number.

(What revclations,
I think then,
If only
I could get through to myself.)

Gerda Mayer

Automobile Mechanics

Sometimes
I help my dad
Work on our automobile.
We unscrew
The radiator cap
And let some water run –
Swish – from a hose
Into the tank.

And then we open up the hood
And feed in oil
From a can with a long spout.
And then we take a lot of rags
And clean all about.
We clean the top
And the doors
And the fenders and the wheels
And the windows and floors . . .
And work hard
My dad
And I.

Dorothy Baruch

I May, I Might, I Must

If you will tell me why the fen
appears impassable, I then
will tell you why I think that I
can get across it if I try.

Marianne Moore

Tich Miller

Tich Miller wore glasses
with elastoplast-pink frames
and had one foot three sizes larger
                  than the other.

When they picked teams for outdoor games
she and I were always the last two
left standing by the wire-mesh fence.

We avoided one another's eyes,
stooping, perhaps, to re-tie a shoelace,
or affecting interest in the flight

of some fortunate bird, and pretended
not to hear the urgent conference:
'Have Tubby!' 'No, no, have Tich!'

Usually they chose me, the lesser dud,
and she lolloped, unselected,
to the back of the other team.

At eleven we went to different schools.
In time I learned to get my own back,
sneering at hockey-players who couldn't spell.

Tich died when she was twelve.

Wendy Cope

Mattie Lou at Twelve

they always said "what a pretty little girl
$$\text{you are}"$$
and she would smile

they always said "how nice of you to help
your mother with your brothers and sisters"
and she would smile and think

they said "what lovely pigtails you have
and you plaited them all by yourself!"
and she would say "thank you"

and they always said "all those Bs
what a good student you are"
and she would smile and say "thank you"

they said "you will make a fine woman
$$\text{some day}"$$
and she would smile and go her way

because she knew

Nikki Giovanni

15

Our Great Secret

When you're thirteen
You have ideas which you can't tell
Anyone, no one, anymore
Not even your parents.
It's a secret you can't tell
Anyone, no one, no more.
They say you're too small
They would not understand
It's a pity they don't understand
Because
It's A Great Secret
Great Secret! Great Secret!

*Bruna Basanese**

I'm so good at archery
I could beat Robin Hood.
It's no lie.
I could even shoot a fly
from a hundred yards away.
I could shoot an arrow to the moon.
No sweat!
I wonder if it's there yet?

*Kate Gage**

Surfboard Life

I'm riding on a surfboard life
someone gave me
a while ago I started out
in the middle of some wavy water
I've been surfing ever since
I fall off
a wave hits me from behind
then there I go
back on that surfing thing
I live on
no land is in sight
the streams of water
spray around me
I balance
the crest is below me
I can't be stopped now

Julie O'Callaghan

Change

The summer
still hangs
heavy and sweet
with sunlight
as it did last year.

The autumn
still comes
showering gold and crimson
as it did last year.

The winter
still stings
clean and cold and white
as it did last year.

The spring
still comes
like a whisper in the dark night.

It is only I
who have changed.

Charlotte Zolotow

Oh, Dearie Me!

O Dearie Me

O dearie me,
Me mother's got a flea,
She put it in the teapot
To make a cup of tea.
The flea jumped out,
Me mother did shout,
In came me brother
With his shirt hanging out.

Traditional

A New Ending for an Old Rhyme

One, two, three –
Mother caught a flea –
Put it in the teapot
And made a cup of tea.
Four, five, six –
The flea's in a fix –
Swimming in the water
And giving final kicks –
Seven, eight, nine,
The flea's doing fine!
We left him for the winter
And turned him into wine –
Get to ten –
And go back again
Ten back to one –
Wasn't that fun?

Sally Farrell Odgers

Over the garden wall
I let the baby fall
My mother came out
And gave me a clout.
She gave me another
To match the other
Over the garden wall

Traditional

Nursery Song

Too-well-done
Has blown out the sun;
She made curdy puddings
Till milk there was none;

And the baby starved
For all he was clean
And the cat ate my thrush
And still looked lean.

Such ugly confusion
There never was seen
Since Too-well-done
Has blown out the sun.

Anna Wickham

Momotara

Where did Momotara go,
With a hoity-toity-tighty?
He went to lay the giants low,
The wicked ones and mighty.

What did Momotara take?
His monkey, dog and pheasant,
Some dumplings and an almond cake,
Which made the journey pleasant.

How did Momotara fare
Upon the fearful meeting?
He seized the giants by the hair
And gave them all a beating.

What did Momotara bring?
Oh, more than you could measure:
A silver coat, a golden ring
And a wagon-load of treasure.

What did Momotara do?
He sat himself astride it;
The monkcy pushed, the pheasant drew
And the little dog ran beside it.

A Japanese nursery rhyme
Translated by Rose Fyleman

The Wise Cow Enjoys a Cloud

"Where did you sleep last night, Wise Cow?
Where did you lay your head?"

"I caught my horns on a rolling cloud
and made myself a bed,

and in the morning ate it raw
on freshly buttered bread."

Nancy Willard

There was an Old Woman Lived under the Stairs

There was an old woman lived under the stairs.
Hee-haw, hee-haw.
She sold apples, and she sold pears.
Hee-haw-hum.

All her bright money she laid on the shelf.
Hee-haw, hee-haw.
If you want any more you can sing it yourself.
Hee-haw-hum.

Traditional

Children children.
Yes, Grandma.
Where have you been?
To see Grandpa.
What did you eat?
Bread and cheese.
Where's my share?
Up in the air.
How will I get it?
Stand on a chair.
What if I fall?
We don't care.

Traditional

Rain A-fall

Rain a-fall, breeze a-blow,
All the washing deh a doah,
Nothing sharp like granny tongue
When breeze blow the wash-line dung.

Valerie Bloom

Elizabeth, Elspeth, Betsy and Bess
They all went together to seek a bird's nest;
They found a bird's nest with five eggs in,
They all took one and left four in.

Traditional

If I wanted to knit a garden
I would cast on
drooping elm
trailing leaf
spiral rib
spider's web
cat's paw
honey comb
shell and shower
open star
snowdrop
seeded chevron
cat's eye
butterfly
arrow lace
or
double moss stitch.

Susanna Steele

Knit the knot: a riddle

The directions said:
to knit the knot known and
not to knit the not known,
knit the knot known
to the unknown knot
and not the knot known to
unknot the unknown
and knot the knit;
to unknot the known and knit
the unknown, unknit the
knot known and know the knit;
to know how to not know
the unknown, knit the knot.
Gnaw your fingers to the bone
until you understand the plot.

Judy Grahn

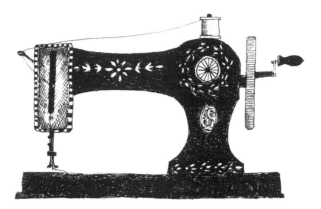

Sewing Machine

I'm faster, I'm faster than fingers,
much faster.
No mistress can match me, no mistress
nor master.
My bobbin is racing to feed in the
thread,
Pink, purple, grey, green, lemon-yellow
or red.
My needle, my needle, my slim, sharp
steel needle.
Makes tiny, neat stitches in trousers
and dresses
And firmly my silver foot presses,
I'm faster, I'm faster than fingers,
much faster.

Gwen Dunn

Continental Lentil Rissole Recipe
Continental Lentil Rissole Recipe
Continental Lentil Rissole Recipe
Continental Lentil Rissole Recipe
Continental Lentil Rissole Recipe
Continental Lentil Rissole Recipe
Continental Lentil Rissole Recipe
Continental Lentil Rissole Recipe
Continental Lentil Rissole Recipe
Continental Lentil Rissole Recipe

Found in the Kitchen

Says she to me
Was thon you
Says I who?
Says she you
Says I where?
Says she there
Says I No
Says she Oh!

Traditional
Ireland

God bless all those that I love;
God bless all those that love me;
God bless all those that love those that I love,
And all those that love those that love me.

Traditional U.S.A.
From an old New England sampler

The Moon and
the Stars Above

The Song of the Sky Loom

O our Mother the Earth, O our Father the Sky,
... weave for us a garment of brightness;
May the warp be the white light of morning,
May the weft be the red light of evening,
May the fringes be the falling rain,
May the border be the standing rainbow.
Thus weave for us a garment of brightness
That we may walk fittingly where birds sing,
That we may walk fittingly where grass is green,
O our Mother the Earth, O our Father the Sky!

Native American, U.S.A.

O Lady Moon, your horns point toward
                              the east:
Shine, be increased;

O Lady Moon, your horns point toward
                              the west:
Wane, be at rest.

Christina Rossetti

Wind and Silver

Greatly shining,
The Autumn moon floats in the sky;
And the fish-ponds shake their backs
      and flash their dragon scales
As she passes over them.

Amy Lowell

Full Moon Rhyme

There's a hare in the moon tonight,
crouching alone in the bright
buttercup field of the moon;
and all the dogs in the world
howl at the hare in the moon.

'I chased that hare to the sky,'
the hungry dogs all cry.
'The hare jumped into the moon
and left me here in the cold.
I chased that hare to the moon.'

'Come down again, mad hare,
we can see you there,'
the dogs all howl to the moon
'Come down again to the world,
you mad black hare in the moon,

or we will grow wings and fly
up to the star-grassed sky
to hunt you out of the moon,'
the hungry dogs of the world
howl at the hare in the moon.

Judith Wright

Starlight,
Starbright.
First star I see tonight,
I wish I may,
I wish I might,
Have this wish I wish tonight.

Traditional

The Falling Star

I saw a star slide down the sky,
Blinding the north as it went by,
Too burning and too quick to hold,
Too lovely to be bought or sold,
Good only to make wishes on
And then forever to be gone.

Sara Teasdale

The Moon

The moon was but a chin of gold
A night or two ago,
And now she turns her perfect face
Upon the world below.

Emily Dickinson

They Should Not Have Left her Alone

They should not have left her alone that night,
To leave her there in the midnight light.

The dry breeze ran through her hair,
The moonbeams shone above, beware.

The dark trees danced to a mysterious beat,
The ground opened beneath her feet.

No-one knows what happened that night,
When she lay all alone in the midnight light.

Sonia Delander*

The Greater Cats

The greater cats with golden eyes
Stare out between the bars.
Deserts are there, and different skies,
And night with different stars.

Vita Sackville-West

Madame Mouse Trots

Madame Mouse trots,
Grey in the black night!
Madame Mouse trots:
furred in the light.
The elephant trunks
Trumpet from the sea . . .
Grey in the black night
The mouse trots free.
Hoarse as a dog's bark
The heavy leaves are furled . . .
The cat's in his cradle,
All's well with the world.

Edith Sitwell

Different Dreams

When dusk is done
And the gray has gone
And the stars blow out
That once were on,
Then the pale moon casts
Its frozen gleams
And the hollow of night
Fills up with dreams:
Cats of mice
Elves of trolls
Cooks of silver spoons and bowls.
Poets dream of winds to Rome.
Sailors dream of ships and home.
Princes dream of foreign lands
To conquer
And of ladies' hands.
Dogs dream dreams
Of hounds and hares
The red fox dreams
Of grass green lairs.
While deep in your sleep
With your dark eyes shut tight,
You dream of the day
That will follow the night.

Karla Kuskin

And the Earth Beneath

The Sun

I praise the disk of the rising sun
red as a parrot's beak, sharp-rayed,
friend of the lotus grove,
an earring from the goddess of the east.

(extract) Traditional, C8th AD, India

In the Sun

Sit
on your doorstep
or any place.

Sit
in the sun
and lift your face.

Close your eyes and
sun dream.
Soon the warm warm sun
will seem
to fill you up
and
spill over.

Lilian Moore

47

On Early Morning

Peach blossom after rain
Is deeper red;
The willow fresher green;
Twittering overhead;
And fallen petals lie wind-blown,
Unswept upon the courtyard stone.

Early Chinese
Translated by Helen Waddell

Little Ellie sits alone
'Mid the beeches of a meadow,
By a stream-side on the grass,
And the trees are showering down
Doubles of their leaves in shadow
On her shining hair and face.

(extract) Elizabeth Barrett Browning

June

The day is warm
and a breeze is blowing,
the sky is blue
and its eye is glowing,
and everything's new
and green and growing . . . .

My shoes are off
and my socks are showing . . . .

My socks are off . . . .

Do you know how I'm going?
　　　BAREFOOT!

Aileen Fisher

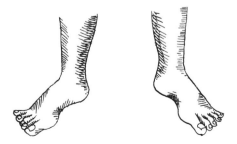

Ladybird! Ladybird!

Ladybird! Ladybird! Fly away home,
Night is approaching, and sunset is come:
The herons are flown to their trees by the Hall;
Felt, but unseen, the damp dewdrops fall.
This is the close of a still summer day;
Ladybird! Ladybird! haste! fly away.

Emily Brontë

An Indian Hymn of Thanks to Mother Corn

See! The Mother Corn comes hither, making all
hearts glad!
Making all hearts glad!
Giving her thanks, she brings a blessing; now,
behold! she is here!

Yonder Mother Corn is coming, coming unto us!
Coming unto us!
Peace and plenty she is bringing; now, behold!
she is here!

Native American, U.S.A.

Sea Timeless Song

Hurricane come
and hurricane go
but sea – sea timeless
sea timeless
sea timeless
sea timeless
see timeless

Hibiscus bloom
then dry-wither so
but sea – sea timeless
sea timeless
sea timeless
sea timeless
sea timeless

Tourist come
and tourist go
but sea – sea timeless
sea timeless
sea timeless
sea timeless
sea timeless

Grace Nichols

Moved

The great sea stirs me.
The great sea sets me adrift,
it sways me like the weed
on a river-stone.

The sky's height stirs me.
The strong wind blows through my mind.
It carries me with it,
So I shake with joy.

Iglukik Woman, Canada
Translated by Tom Lowenstein

Wild Geese

I heard the wild geese flying
In the dead of the night,
With beat of wings and crying
I heard the wild geese flying,
And dreams in my heart sighing
Followed their northward flight.
I heard the wild geese flying
In the dead of the night.

Elinor Chipp

Something Told the Wild Geese

Something told the wild geese
It was time to go.
Though the fields lay golden
Something whispered, "Snow."
Leaves were green and stirring,
Berries, luster-glossed,
But beneath warm feathers
Something cautioned, "Frost."
All the sagging orchards
Steamed with amber spice,
But each wild breast stiffened
At remembered ice.
Something told the wild geese
It was time to fly —
Summer sun was on their wings,
Winter in their cry.

Rachel Field

November Night

Listen . . . . .
With faint dry sound,
Like steps of passing ghosts,
The leaves, frost-crisped, break from the trees
And fall.

Adelaide Crapsey

So Will I

My grandfather remembers long ago
the white Queen Anne's lace that grew wild.
He remembers the buttercups and goldenrod
from when he was a child.

He remembers long ago
the white snow falling falling.
He remembers the bluebird and thrush
at twilight
calling, calling.

He remembers long ago
the new moon in the summer sky
He remembers the wind in the trees
and its long, rising sigh.
And so will I
So will I.

Charlotte Zolotow

For Grandma's Sake, Hush up

Grandma's Lullaby

Close your eyes,
My precious love,
Grandma's little
Turtledove.

Go to sleep now,
Pretty kitty,
Grandma's little
Chickabiddy.

Stop your crying,
Cuddly cutie,
Grandma's little
Sweet patootie.

Issum, wissum,
Popsy wopsy,
Tootsie wootsie
Lollypopsie.
Diddims
Huggle
Snuggle pup

And now, for Grandma's sake, hush up!

Charlotte Pomerantz

Lullaby

Sleep, my baby, the night is coming soon.
Sleep, my baby, the day has broken down.

Sleep now: let silence come, let the shadows
                                    form
A castle of strength for you, a fortress of calm.

You are so small, sleep will come with ease.
Hush now, be still now, join the silences.

Elizabeth Jennings

My Daughter

My necklace of precious stones
    You are turquoise
    you are jade
    you are feather

You are my blood
you are my colour
you are my image

     listen my child
     understand my child

You are alive
you're born
    come close to me
    listen!

(extract) Traditional Mexico
Translated by Toni de Gerez

A Highland Lullaby

I left my baby lying there,
Lying there, lying there,
I left my baby lying there,
To go and gather blaeberries.

Hovan hovan gorry og o,
Gorry og o, gorry og o,
Hovan hovan gorry og o,
But never found my baby-o.

I saw the wee brown otter's track,
Otter's track, otter's track,
I saw the wee brown otter's track,
But never found my baby-o.

Chorus

I saw the swan's nest on the loch,
On the loch, on the loch,
I saw the swan's nest on the loch,
But never found my baby-o.

Chorus

I saw the track of the yellow deer,
Yellow deer, yellow deer,
I saw the track of the yellow deer,
But never found my baby-o.

Chorus

I heard the curlew crying high,
Crying high, crying high,
I heard the curlew crying high,
But never found my baby-o.

Traditional Scotland

All the Pretty Little Horses

Hushaby
Don't you cry,
Go to sleep, little baby,
When you wake,
You shall have,
All the pretty little horses –
Blacks and bays,
Dapples and grays,
Coach and six-a little horses.
Hushaby,
Don't you cry,
Go to sleep, little baby.

Traditional USA

Lullaby

Someone would like to have you as her child
But you are mine.
Somcone would like to rear you on a costly mat
But you are mine.
Someone would like to place you on a camel
                                    blanket
But you are mine.
I have you to rear on a torn old mat,
Someone would like to have you as her child
But you are mine.

Akan Woman
Traditional Africa

A Welcome Song for Laini Nzinga

Born November 24, 1975

Hello, little Sister.
Coming through the rim of the world.
We are here! to meet you and to mould and to
maintain you.
With excited eyes we see you.
With welcoming ears we hear the
clean sound of new language.
The language of Laini Nzinga.
We love and we receive you as our own.

Gwendolyn Brooks

Ruth is Six

A mobile floats above her bed
Of fishes, green and grey,
That move on drifting waves of air
As night gives place to day.

And Ruth, her eyes still dimmed with sleep,
Lies blissfully aware
Of her lazy mermaid's waving tail,
And seaweed through her hair.

Lydia Pender

63

The Bed Book

Most Beds are Beds
For sleeping or resting,
but the *best* Beds are much
More interesting!

Not just a white little
Tucked-in-tight little
Nighty-night little
Turn-out-the-light little
BED.

(extract) Sylvia Plath

Mother Worm's Hum

Sleep, young wriggler,
Under your grass coverlet,
Under your earth sheet.
Do not be surprised to find
That morning is just as dark.

Jane Yolen

Telling Tales

The Meanings in the Pattern

The interior of the Arizona Indian museum
is cool. A woman stands at the counter,
selling her family wares. "I am a Pima,"
she says. "We have always been here.
People say, where did the Anasazi go?
But we are right here, we never left.
We were farmers, always.
We were promised water for our gardens,
now they are taking it. My daughter
made the baskets; only girls are taught
to do it. My son made this pouch."
She pats the small soft leather purse,
thick with close beading, red and white,
yellow and blue. The design: clouds,
a bird, a man, the earth.
"This picture tells a story," she says.
Her black eyes looking inward and outward.
"No one who buys this could ever understand —
the meanings in the pattern. What it is
really worth." Clouds. A
bird. A man. Her fingers
feel the beads. "There is a story here.
It takes three days and nights to tell it."

Judy Grahn

Magic Story of Falling Asleep

When the last giant came out of his cave
and his bones turned into the mountain
and his clothes turned into the flowers,

nothing was left but his tooth
which my dad took home in his truck
which my granddad carved into a bed

which my mum tucks me into at night
when I dream of the last giant
when I fall asleep on the mountain.

Nancy Willard

The Witch

I have walked a great while over the snow,
And I am not tall nor strong.
My clothes are wet, and my teeth are set,
And the way was hard and long.
I have wandered over the fruitful earth,
But I never came here before.
Oh, lift me over the threshold,
      and let me in at the door!

The cutting wind is a cruel foe.
I dare not stand in the blast.
My hands are stone, and my voice a groan,
And the worst of death is past.
I am but a little maiden still,
My little white feet are sore.
Oh, lift me over the threshold,
      and let me in at the door!

Her voice was the voice that women have,
Who plead for their heart's desire.
She came – she came – and the quivering flame
Sank and died in the fire.
It never was lit again on my hearth
Since I hurried across the floor,
To lift her over the threshold,
      and let her in at the door.

Mary Coleridge
C19th

I Like to Stay Up

I like to stay up
and listen
when big people talking
jumbie stories

I does feel
so tingly and excited
inside me

But when my mother say
'Girl, time for bed'

Then is when
I does feel a dread

Then is when
I does jump into me bed

Then is when
I does cover up
from me feet to me head

Then is when
I does wish I didn't listen
to no stupid jumbie story

Then is when
I does wish I did read
me book instead

Grace Nichols

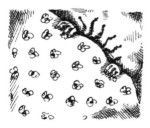

('Jumbie' is a Guyanese word for 'ghost')

The Bean-Stalk

Ho, Giant! This is I!
I have built me a bean-stalk into your sky!
La, — but it's lovely, up so high!

This is how I came, — I put
Here my knee, there my foot,
Up and up, from shoot to shoot —
And the blessèd bean-stalk thinning
Like the mischief all the time,
Till it took me rocking, spinning,
In a dizzy, sunny circle,
Making angles with the root,
Far and out above the cackle
Of the city I was born in,
Till the little dirty city
In the light so sheer and sunny
Shone as dazzling bright and pretty
As the money that you find
In a dream of finding money —
What a wind! What a morning! —

Till the tiny, shiny city,
When I shot a glance below,
Shaken with a giddy laughter,
Sick and blissfully afraid,
Was a dew-drop on a blade,
And a pair of moments after

Was the whirling guess I made, —
And the wind was like a whip
Cracking past my icy ears,

And my hair stood out behind,
And my eyes were full of tears,
Wide-open and cold,
More tears than they could hold,
The wind was blowing so,
And my teeth were in a row,
Dry and grinning,
And I felt my foot slip,
And I scratched the wind and whined,
And I clutched the stalk and jabbered,
With my eyes shut blind, —
What a wind! What a wind!

Your broad sky, Giant,
Is the shelf of a cupboard;
I make bean-stalks, I'm
A builder, like yourself,
But bean-stalks is my trade,
I couldn't make a shelf,
Don't know how they're made,
Now, a bean-stalk is more pliant —
La, what a climb!

Edna St. Vincent Millay

73

Cinema

Special Saturday
Half-price matinée,
Grandma's holiday.

She likes to tell it out to us
Spell it out to us –
How she loved to go
To a show
Long ago.

And all about
The sweet scented
Faded
Gold-painted
Fusty
Dusty
Screen dream
Massive screen . . .
Rainbow dream . . .

"Fifty years ago this was a palace!
            (said my grandmother)
A glass and chromium
Theatre Organolean
Would rise
To the skies
In a flickering
Gilt glittering
Criss-crossing of coloured light spots –
And Boom . . . !
Through the Gloom . . . (said my
                    grandmother)"

I wish I could have seen it when
It was all plush and gold;
Now it just looks old –
But it must have been a palace then,
Just as grandma told.

Marion Lines

City-Under-Water

Maureen came out of Ireland with her
                double-cutting tongue.
She was crusty with the older folk,
                but easy with the young.
She gave my Mother answers back my Mother
                thought too free,
But Maureen gave nothing else but songs
                and fairy tales to me.

She told me of a lovely lake – in her own land,
                she said –
With a City-Under-Water lying sunken
                on its bed.
Sometimes, she said, you'd surely hear the
                church-bells ringing good
And clear right from the bottom to the top,
                indeed you would.

She tucked me in and left me after pulling up
                the blind,
And City-Under-Water kept on running
                in my mind.
She pulled my blind because, if I was anything
                like *her*,
I'd find the stars were worth considering,
                indeed they were.

I looked out through the window where the
                        stars looked in again,
And the sky spread like a dark blue lake across
                        the window-pane.
I thought that I was looking down instead of
                        looking up,
And the silver stars were swarming at the
                        bottom of a cup.

I saw bright spires and shining streets
                        and tall and glittering towers,
And trees with silver cherries on, and silver
                        cherry-flowers,
And silver swallows flying where the silver
                        fishes slid,
And silver churchbells ringing good and clear,
                        indeed they did.

Next day I told my Mother, and I told
                        my Maureen too,
I'd seen City-Under-Water. Mother said
                        it wasn't true,
I'd had a dream. But *Maureen* said, sure, did I
                        think because
I'd dreamed about a thing it wasn't true?
                        Indeed it was.

Eleanor Farjeon

The Ballad of the Great Bear

When Zeus was king of the gods
    and Hera was queen,
There was a land called Arcady
    of wild woods and green.

And nymphs played in the deep glades
    where few strangers came.
The fairest nymph in Arcady,
    Kallisto was her name.

One day, and she was hunting,
    Zeus saw her there,
And he loved her for her bold step
    and the white ribbon in her hair.

Queen Hera paced the cold halls.
    Cruel was her frown.
"My husband gone with a wood-nymph –
    and now she's borne him a son!

"And she be unpunished?
    This day I'll go
And pay her a visit in Arcady –
    and no mercy show!"

In the deep woods she found her.
She threw her to the ground.
"Say good-bye to your beauty, girl!"
"Mercy!" Kallisto moaned.

But her skin began prickling.
with hairs thick as grass.
She saw her hands curved round
into crooked claws.

Now she begged *Mercy*
a growl grazed the air
From a mouth grown to gaping jaws –
the jaws of a bear.

A great bear roams Arcady,
the long years roll by.
Nothing but fear and loneliness
to keep her company.

One day a boy came hunting,
his spear still untried.
"Now winter's in the air, I need
a good bear-hide."

The bear stood gazing at his face.
A strange growl he heard.
It's your son! her eyes told her.
She could not say a word.

Zeus glanced from his high tower.
    Then pity felt he.
"My son kill his mother – No,
    this must not be!"

He spun the air about them
    to a whirlwind wild.
Far up through the sky it carried
    mother and child.

In the dark depths of space glimmered
    one star's bright bead
When a swarm of lights sprang up beside,
    like scattered seed.

Nightlong over Arcady
    their pale fires burned.
Unchanging in their pattern
    they turned as the world turned.

Then, now – for ever,
    while earth's seasons run –
Still their slow circle tread
    the Great Bear, and her son.

Libby Houston

Persephone

Lay down your poppies
   red with sun,
   beneath the judas-tree;
   beware the black-horsed lord of night,
   Persephone.

Bury your violets
   with the shades,
   drink deep the black, black sea;
   ferry your corn to Dis's cave,
   Persephone.

Fasten your veil with
   lilies pale,
   dull nightshade dim your eyes;
   under sad lilac make your grave,
   till winter dies.

Judith Nicholls

Hollyhocks

Hollyhocks stand in clumps
By the doors of old cottages.

Even when one springs alone,
Lost, in an uncut field,

It builds beside it the cottage,
The garden, the old woman, the beehive.

Valerie Worth

When maidens are young and in their spring,
    Of pleasure, of pleasure,
Let 'em take their full swing,
    Full swing, full swing,
And love and dance, and play, and sing.

For Silvia, believe it, when youth is done,
There's naught but hum-drum, hum-drum,
    hum-drum,
There's naught but hum-drum, hum-drum,
    hum-drum.

Aphra Behn
C17th

Overheard in County Sligo

I married a man from County Roscommon
and I live at the back of beyond
with a field of cows and a yard of hens
and six white geese on the pond.

At my door's a square of yellow corn
caught up by its corners and shaken,
and the road runs down through the open gate
and freedom's there for the taking.

I had thought to work on the Abbey stage
or have my name in a book,
to see my thought on the printed page,
or still the crowd with a look.

But I turn to fold the breakfast cloth
and to polish the lustre and brass,
to order and dust the tumbled rooms
and find my face in the glass.

I ought to feel I'm a happy woman
for I lie in the lap of the land,
and I married a man from County Roscommon
and I live in the back of beyond.

Gillian Clarke

Song

The world is full of coloured
people
People of Colour
Tra-la-la
The world is full of
coloured people
Tra-la-la-la-la.

They have black hair
and black and brown
eyes
The world is full of
coloured people
Tra-la-la.

The world is full of coloured
people
People of Colour
Tra-la-la
The world is full of coloured
people
Tra-la-la-la-la.

Their skins are pink and yellow
and brown
All coloured people
People of Colour
Coloured people
Tra-la-la

Some have full lips
Some have thin
Full of coloured people
People of Colour
Coloured lips
Tra-la-la.

The world is full of
coloured people
People of Colour
Colourful people
Tra-la-la!

Alice Walker

Father Grumble

There was an old man who lived in the wood,
As you can plainly see.
Who said he could do more work in one day,
Than his wife could do in three.
'If that be true' the woman said,
'Why then you must allow,
That you shall do my work for one day
While I go drive the plough.'

'But you must milk the tiny cow
For fear she should go dry,
And you must feed the little pigs
That are within the sty;
And you must watch the bracket hen
Lest she should lay astray
And you must wind the reel of yarn
That I spun yesterday.'

The old woman took the staff in her hand
And went to drive the plough;
The old man took the pail in his hand
And went to milk the cow.
But Tiny hitched and Tiny flitched
And Tiny cocked her nose
And Tiny gave the man such a kick
The blood ran to his toes.

And when he had milked the tiny cow
For fear she should go dry,
Why, then he fed the little pigs
That were within the sty.
And then he watched the bracket hen
Lest she should lay astray;
But he forgot the reel of yarn
His wife spun yesterday.

He swore by all the stars in heaven
And leaves upon the tree,
His wife could do more work in a day
Than he could do in three.
By all the leaves upon the tree
And all the stars in heaven –
His wife could do more work in a day
Than he could do in seven!

Traditional

The Builders

I told them a thousand times if I told them once:
Stop fooling around, I said, with straw and sticks;
They won't hold up; you're taking an awful chance.
Brick is the stuff to build with, solid bricks.
You want to be impractical, go ahead.
But just remember, I told them; wait and see,
You're making a big mistake. Awright, I said,
But when the wolf comes, don't come running to me.

The funny thing is, they didn't. There they sat,
One in his crummy yellow shack, and one
Under his roof of twigs, and the wolf ate
Them, hair and hide. Well, what is done is done.
But I'd been willing to help them, all along,
If only they'd once admitted they were wrong.

Sara Henderson Hay

Noo my story's endit
And gin ye be offendit,
Tak a needle and threid
And sew a bit t' end o't.

(gin — if)

Traditional, Scotland

Wha Me Mudder Do

Wha Me Mudder Do

Mek me tell you wha me Mudder do
wha me mudder do
wha me mudder do

Me mudder pound plantain mek fufu
Me mudder catch crab mek calaloo stew

Mek me tell you wha me mudder do
wha me mudder do
wha me mudder do

Me mudder beat hammer
Me mudder turn screw
she paint chair red
then she paint it blue

Mek me tell you wha me mudder do
wha me mudder do
wha me muddcr do

Me mudder chase bad-cow
with one 'Shoo'
she paddle down river
in she own canoe
Ain't have nothing
dat me mudder can't do
Ain't have nothing
dat me mudder can't do

Mek me tell you

Grace Nichols

Sugarfields

treetalk and windsong
are the language of my mother
her music does not leave me.

let me taste again the cane
the syrup of the earth
sugarfields were once my home.

I would lie down in the fields
and never get up again
(treetalk and windsong
are the language of my mother
sugarfields are my home)

the leaves go on whispering secrets
as the wind blows a tune in the grass
my mother's voice is in the fields
this music cannot leave me.

Barbara Mahone

Three Poems for Women

This is a poem for a woman doing dishes.
This is a poem for a woman doing dishes.
It must be repeated.
It must be repeated,
again and again,
again and again,
because the woman doing dishes
because the woman doing dishes
has trouble hearing
has trouble hearing.

And this is another poem for a woman
cleaning the floor
who cannot hear at all.
Let us have a moment of silence
for the woman who cleans the floor.

And here is one more poem
for the woman at home
with children.
You never see her at night.
Stare at an empty space and imagine her there,
the woman with children
because she cannot be here to speak
for herself,
and listen
to what you think
she might say.

Susan Griffin

Folding Sheets

They must be clean.
There ought to be two of you
to talk as you work, your
eyes and hands meeting.
They can be crisp, a little rough
and fragrant from the line;
or hot from the dryer
as from the oven. A silver
grey kitten with amber
eyes to dart among
the sheets and wrestle and leap out
helps. But mostly pleasure
lies in the clean linen
slapping into shape.
Whenever I fold a fitted sheet
making the moves that are like
closing doors, I feel my mother.
The smell of clean laundry is hers.

Marge Piercey

I Haven't Had a Pair of Shorts

I haven't had a pair of shorts
since I was ten and passing
for pleasingly chubby.

Years later, I know
it's my mother's fault.

So I bought a pair of shorts and
I said to my mother, hey mum, guess what,
I've bought a pair of shorts.

And my mother, now sixty-seven,
said to me, well that's nice, dear,
I expect they'll be cool for the summer.

Now, where was I?

C M Donald

Clean New Dirty Old Jeans

I like jeans
blue jeans
new jeans
old jeans
gold jeans
jeans with purple polka dots

Jeans with giraffes on 'em
Jeans with lions
Jeans with elephants even
Jeans that have flies

Jeans with pockets
Jeans with rockets
Jeans with snotty comebacks on 'em

Clean jeans
painty jeans
perfectly good jeans
raggedy jeans
baggy jeans

Like I said:
new blue jeans
But best of all: old jeans
– grubby raggedy old jeans
that Mama and Papa and Grandma and Grandpa
and our school principle Harold Nyquist
just can't stand.

Siv Widerberg

For my Grandmother Knitting

There is no need they say
but the needles still move
their rhythms in the working of your hands
as easily
as if your hands
were once again those sure and skilful hands
of the fisher-girl.

You are old now
and your grasp of things is not so good
but master of your moments then
deft and swift
you slit the still-ticking quick silver fish.
Hard work it was too
of necessity.

But now they say there is no need
as the needles move
in the working of your hands
once the hands of the bride
with the hand-span waist
once the hands of the miner's wife
who scrubbed his back
in a tin bath by the coal fire
once the hands of the mother
of six who made do and mended
scraped and slaved slapped sometimes
when necessary.

But now they say there is no need
the kids they say grandma
have too much already
more than they can wear
too many scarves and cardigans –
gran you do too much
there's no neccessity.

At your window you wave
them goodbye Sunday.
With your painful hands
big on shrunken wrists.
Swollen-jointed. Red. Arthritic. Old.
But the needles still move
their rhythms in the working of your hands
easily
as if your hands remembered
of their own accord the pattern
as if your hands had forgotten
how to stop.

Liz Lochhead

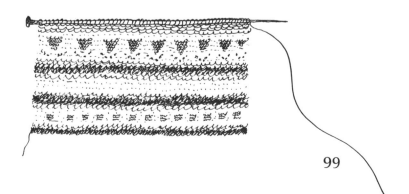

Granny Granny Please Comb my Hair

Granny Granny please comb
my hair
you always take your time
you always take such care

You put me on a cushion
between your knees
you rub a little coconut oil
parting gentle as a breeze

Mummy Mummy
she's always in a hurry-hurry
rush
she pulls my hair
sometimes she tugs

But Granny
you have all the time
in the world
and when you're finished
you always turn my head and say
'Now who's a nice girl'

Grace Nichols

I keep a photo of my Grandmother.
I have never seen my Grandmother.
I keep a photo of her
in my rose box.
My Grandmother
sitting on a chair
in the garden.

*Sau Yee Kan**

Evening star! You bring back
All that the bright dawn scattered;
You bring back the sheep to the fold
That wandered all day on the hillside.
You bring back the goat, and you bring
The child back home to its mother.

Sappho/Early Greece
Translated by Beram Saklatvala

Where are those Songs?

Where are those songs
my mother and yours
always sang
fitting rhythms
to the whole
vast span of life?

What was it again
they sang
    harvesting maize, threshing millet,
            storing the grain . . .

What did they sing
bathing us, rocking us to sleep . . .
and the one they sang
stirring the pot
(swallowed in parts by choking smoke)?

What was it
the woods echoed
as in long file
my mother and yours and all the women
                on our ridge
beat out the rhythms
    trudging gaily
    as they carried
    piles of wood
    through those forests
    miles from home

What song was it?

And the row of bending women
hoeing our fields
to what beat
did they
break the stubborn ground
as they weeded
our *shambas*?

What did they sing
at the ceremonies
   child-birth
   child-naming
   second birth
   initiation. . .?
how did they trill the *ngemi*
what was
the warriors' song?
how did the wedding song go?
sing me
the funeral song.

What do you remember?

Sing
   I have forgotten
   my mother's song
   my children
   will never know.

This I remember:

Mother always said
    sing child sing
    make a song
    and sing
    beat out your own rhythms
    the rhythms of your life
    but make the song soulful
    and make life
    sing

Sing daughter sing
around you are
uncountable tunes
some sung
others unsung
sing them
to your rhythms
observe
listen
absorb
soak yourself
bathe
in the stream of life
    and then sing
    sing
    simple songs
    for the people
    for all to hear
    and learn
    and sing
    with you

Micere Mugo   105

Mother

I have a happy nature,
But Mother is always sad,
I enjoy every moment of my life, —
Mother has been had.

Stevie Smith

And a New Day Calling

Clockface

Hours pass
slowly as a snail
creeping between the grassblades
of the minutes.

Judith Thurman

No One Can Call Me

Here is my heaven – on the top of a bus.
I gaze down on the no-time world.
People hurry along pavements:
women with shopping-bags and children;
men with brief-cases.
No time to look at one another
because their eyes are on the clock.
No clock to see but they feel it,
feel its hands pulling them along
away from now,
pulling them away from themselves,
making their minds its mainspring.

Here, up a stairway out of time,
I am my real self in a real world.
No one can call me, catch me –
I am not there.
Ideas are stirring underground
pushing up green shoots into the sun –
I'm wrapped in sun in this plate-glass corner.
There are three of us
travelling alone, coming back to ourselves
on the top of a double-decker bus.

Phoebe Hesketh

Witch

There was this old lady on the bus . . .
          (Old cat! Sourpuss!)
Gave her my hand to pull her on.
"OK, love . . . let me help you, Gran."
But she hissed and spat like a real old mog . . .
Eye of newt and toe of frog.
(She wasn't a bit like my old Nan
Who smells of cake and apple jam.)
If she'd lived two hundred years ago
They'd have ducked her for a witch, you know.

But then I thought . . . If her life's been rough,
          Why – that's enough
          To make her tough . . .
          . . . and spitefulhard.
You never can *really* tell, you see –
In sixty years that might be me.

Marion Lines

On Ageing

When you see me sitting quietly,
Like a sack left on the shelf,
Don't think I need your chattering.
I'm listening to myself.
Hold! Stop! Don't pity me!
Hold! Stop you sympathy!
Understanding if you got it,
Otherwise I'll do without it!

When my bones are stiff and aching
And my feet won't climb the stair,
I will only ask one favour:
Don't bring me no rocking chair.

When you see me walking, stumbling,
Don't study and get it wrong.
'Cause tired don't mean lazy
And every goodbye ain't gone.
I'm the same person I was back then,
A little less hair, a little less chin,
A lot less lungs and much less wind.
But ain't I lucky I can still breathe in.

Maya Angelou

Monument

A person –
a lady –
told me,
'Always ripen
peaches
in a paper bag.'
I think of her
every time
I eat one.
All summer.
Every year.

Felice Holman

Never More Will the Wind

Never more will the wind
cherish you again,
never more will the rain.

Never more
shall we find you bright
in the snow and wind.

The snow is melted,
the snow is gone,
and you are flown:

Like a bird out of our hand,
like a light out of our heart,
you are gone.

Hilda Doolittle (H.D.)

Socks

Shining pins that dart and click
In the fireside's sheltered peace
Check the thoughts that cluster thick —
20 plain and then decrease.

He was brave — well, so was I —
Keen and merry, but his lip
Quivered when he said good-bye —
Purl the seam-stitch, purl and slip.

Never used to living rough,
Lots of things he'd got to learn;
Wonder if he's warm enough —
Knit 2, catch 2, knit 1, turn.

Hark! The paper boys again!
Wish that shout could be suppressed;
Keeps one always on the strain —
Knit off 9, and slip the rest.

Wonder if he's fighting now,
What he's done an' where he's been;
He'll come out on top, somehow —
Slip 1, knit 2, purl 14.

Jessie Pope

Lance-Corporal Dixon

I saw a picture in the paper the other day
Of a soldier carrying a baby.
Lance-corporal Dixon was his name.
The baby?
His CO's daughter.
My mother was touched by the picture,
Said it was charming
That a man so tough
Could be so gentle.
It looked odd to me:
A sten gun under one arm,
A baby under the other.

Linda Newton

Terezin

The heaviest wheel rolls across our foreheads
To bury itself deep somewhere inside our
                                    memories.

We've suffered here more than enough,
Here in this clot of grief and shame,
Wanting a badge of blindness
To be a proof for their own children.

A fourth year of waiting, like standing above
                                    a swamp
From which any moment might gush forth
                                    a spring.

Meanwhile, the rivers flow another way,
Another way,
Not letting you die, not letting you live.

And the cannons don't scream and the guns
                                    don't bark
And you don't see blood here.
Nothing, only silent hunger.
Children steal the bread here and ask and ask
and ask
And all would wish to sleep, keep silent and
just to go to sleep again . . .

The heaviest wheel rolls across our foreheads
To bury itself deep somewhere inside our
                                    memories.

A child's poem from a Concentration Camp 1944

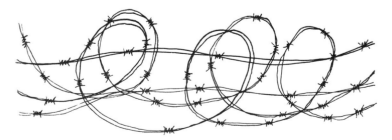

Fantasia

I dream
of
giving birth
to
a child
who will ask,
'Mother,
what was war?'

Eve Merriam

Dawn Wail for the Dead

Dim light of daybreak now
Faintly over the sleeping camp.
Old lubra first to wake remembers:
First thing every dawn
Remember the dead, cry for them.
Softly at first her wail begins,
One by one as they wake and hear,
Join in the cry, and the whole camp
Wails for the dead, the poor dead
Gone from here to the Dark Place:
They are remembered.
Then it is over, life now,
Fires lit, laughter now,
And a new day calling.

Oodgeroo of the tribe Noonuccal
(formerly Kath Walker)

Hold Fast your Dreams

Hold Fast your Dreams

Within your heart
Keep one still, secret spot
Where dreams may go,
And sheltered so,
May thrive and grow –
Where doubt and fear are not.
Oh, keep a place apart
Within your heart,
For little dreams to go.

Louise Driscoll

The Grey Thread

My life is a grey thread,
A thin grey stretched out thread,
And when I trace its course, I moan:
How dull! How dead!

But I have gay beads.
A pale one to begin,
A blue one for my painted dreams,
And one for sin,
Gold with coiled marks,
Like a snake's skin.

For love an odd bead
With a deep purple glow;
A green bead for a secret thing
That few shall know;
And yellow for my thoughts
That melt like snow.

A red bead for my strength,
And crimson for my hate;
Silver for the songs I sing
When I am desolate;
And white for my laughter
That mocks trickster fate.

My life is a grey thread
Stretching through Time's day;
But I have slipped gay, gorgeous beads on it
To hide the grey.

Elsa Gidlow

To Olga

Listen!
The boat whistle has sounded now
And we must sail
Out toward an unknown port.

We'll sail a long, long way
And dreams will turn to truth.
Oh, how sweet the name Morocco!
Listen!
Now it's time.

The wind sings songs of far away,
Just look up to heaven
And think about the violets.

Listen!
Now it's time.

Alena Synkova

A Saying from Zimbabwe

If you can walk
You can dance
If you can talk
You can sing

Traditional Zimbabwe

Speech to the Young

Say to them,
say to the down-keepers,
the sun-slappers,
the self-soilers,
the harmony-hushers,
"Even if you are not ready for day
it cannot always be night."
You will be right.
For that is the hard home-run.

Live not for battles won,
Live not for the-end-of-the-song.
Live in the along.

Gwendolyn Brooks

Index of Poems

125

Traditional poems

Acknowledgements

We are grateful to the following for permission to reproduce copyright material: **W.H. Allen & Co Ltd** for 'Moved' from *Eskimo Poems* translated by Tom Lowenstein. **Angus & Robertson** for 'Ruth is Six' from *Morning Magpie* by Lydia Pender. **Angus & Robertson/Collins** for 'Full Moon Rhyme' by Judith Wright from *Collected Poems 1942–1970*. © Judith Wright 1971. **Bruna Basanese** for 'Our Great Secret' from *Poets in Schools*, Alastair Aston, Harrap, 1977. **Valerie Bloom** for 'Rain a-fall'. **Branden Publishing Company**, Boston, USA, for 'Wild Geese' by Elinor Chipp. **Gwendolyn Brooks** for 'A Welcome Song for Laini Nzinga' & 'Speech to the Young', Third World Press. **Carcanet Press Ltd** for 'Overheard in County Sligo' by Gillian Clarke from *Selected Poems*, 1985. **Cheryl** for 'My Life'. **Constable Publishers** for 'On Early Morning' translated by Helen Waddell from *Lyrics from the Chinese*. **Curtis Brown Ltd** on behalf of Grace Nicols for 'Granny Granny Please Comb my Hair', 'I Like to Stay Up', 'Sea Timeless Song' and 'Wha Me Mudder Do'. © 1988 Grace Nichols; 'The Greater Cats' by Vita Sackville West from *Spokesman: Four Feet plus Two*, Penguin. **The C.W. Daniel Company** for 'Terezin' a child's poem & 'To Olga' by Alena Synkova from *I Never Saw Another Butterfly*, Spearman, 1965. **Sonia Delander** for 'They Should Not Have Left her Alone'. **Gwen Dunn** for 'Sewing Machine'. **Faber & Faber Ltd** for 'I May, I Might, I Must' from the *Complete Poems of Marianne Moore*; 'Tich Miller' from *Making Cocoa for Kingsley Amis* by Wendy Cope; 'Persephone' from *Midnight Forest* by Judith Nicholls. **Farrar, Straus and Giroux, Inc** for 'Hollyhocks' from *Small Poems* Valerie Worth. © 1972 by Valerie Worth. **The Feminist Press at The City University of New York** for 'Clean New Dirty Old Blue Jeans' & 'The Photograph' from *I'm Like Me* by Siv Widerberg. © 1971 Siv Widerberg. Translation © by Verne Moberg. All rights reserved. **Kate Gage** for 'I'm so good at Archery'. **Elsa Gidlow** for 'The Grey Thread' & 'You Say' from *Saphic Songs*, Druid Height Books. **Judy Grahn** for 'Knit the Knot: a Riddle' & 'The Meanings in the Pattern' from *The Queen of Wands*, The Crossing Press. **Susan Griffin** for 'Three Poems for Women' from *In the Pink: the Raving Beauties*, The Women's Press Ltd. **Hamlyn Publishing Group Ltd** for 'Socks' by Jessie Pope from *Scars Upon My Heart*, Catherine Reilley, Virago. **Harper & Row, Publishers, Inc** for 'Different Dreams' from *Dogs and Dragons, Trees and Dreams*, originally in *A Rose On My Cake*. © 1964 by Karla Kuskin. **Sara Henderson Hay** for 'The Builders' from *Reflections on a Gift of Watermelon Pickle*, Dunning, Luendon & Smith, 1967. **A.M. Heath & Co Ltd** for 'Folding Sheets', by Marge Piercey from *My Mother's Body* first pub'd in the US by Alfred Knopf Inc, Random House, 1985, and in the UK by Pandora Press, 1985; 'The Wise Cow Enjoys a Cloud' from *A Visit to William Blake's Inn* by Nancy Willard, Methuen. **Heinemann Ltd** for 'Change' & 'So Will I' by Charlotte Zolotow from *River Winding*; 'June' by Aileen Fisher from *I Wonder How, I Wonder Who*, 1963. **Heinemann Educational Books (Caribbean) Ltd** for a section from 'Protest poem for all the brothers' by Pamela Mordecai from *Jamaica Woman*, Pamela Mordecai & Mervyn Morris, 1980. **Phoebe Hesketh** for 'No One Can Call Me' from *A Song of Sunlight*, Bodley Head. **David Higham Associates Ltd** for 'Lullaby' by Elizabeth Jennings from *The Secret Brother*, Macmillan; 'Madam Mouse Trots' by Edith Sitwell from *Collected Poems*, Macmillan; 'Song' by Alice Walker from *Horses Make A Landscape Look More Beautiful*, The Women's Press; 'City-Under-Water' by Eleanor Farjeon from *Invitation to a Mouse*, Pelham Books. **Hill and Wang, a division of Farrar, Straus and Giroux** for 'Mattie Lou at Twelve' from *Spin a Soft Black Song* by Nikki Giovanni. © 1971 Nikki Giovanni. **Felice Holman Valen** for 'Monument' from *At the Top of My Voice*, Charles Scribner & Sons, New York, 1970. **Libby Houston** for 'The Ballad of the Great Bear'. © Libby Houston, originally commissioned and published by BBC Schools Radio for the series 'Pictures in Your Mind', 1984. **Olwyn Hughes** for an excerpt from 'The Bed Book' by Sylvia Plath, Faber & Faber Ltd. © Ted Hughes 1976. **Sau Yee Kan** for 'I Keep a Photo of my Grandmother'. **Bertha Klausner International Literary Agency, Inc**, New York, for 'Automobile Mechanics' from Dorothy Barach's *I Like Machinery*. **Trang Ly** for her poem 'When I am angry'. **James MacGibbon**, Stevie Smith's executor, for 'Mother' from *The Collected Poems of Stevie Smith*, Penguin Modern Classics. **Macmillan Publishing Company**, New York, for 'Something Told the Wild Geese' from *Branches Green* by Rachel Field. © 1934 Macmillan Publishing Company, 1962 Arthur S Penderson; 'Falling Star' by Sara Teasdale from *Mirror of the Heart*, William Drake, 1984. **Barbara Mahone** for 'Sugarfields' from *The Poetry of Black*

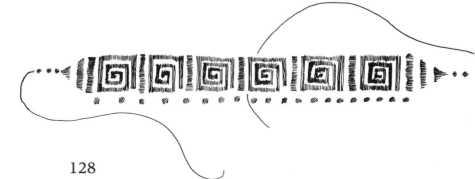